P9-CCY-194

animal babies
in rain forests

KINGFISHER

a Houghton Mifflin Company imprint
222 Berkeley Street
Boston, Massachusetts 02116
www.houghtonmifflinbooks.com

First published in 2004
10 9 8 7 6 5 4 3 2 1

BAF/0506/TWP/PICA(PICA)/150STORA/F

Copyright © Kingfisher Publications Plc 2004

LIBRARY OF CONGRESS CATALOGING-IN-PUBLIATION DATA
Schofield, Jennifer.
    Rain forest / Jennifer Schofield.—1st ed.
        p. cm.—(Animal Babies)
    On board pages.
    Summary: A simple introduction to the baby and adult
    animals that live in the rain forest.
    1. Rain forest animals—Juvenile literature. 2. Animals—
    Infancy—Juvenile literature. [1.
    Rain forest animals. 2. Animals—Infancy.] 1. Title.

QL112.S36 2004
591.734—dc22   2003061911

ISBN 0-7534-5788-1
ISBN 978-0-7534-5788-7

Author and Editor: Jennifer Schofield
Coordinating Editor: Caitlin Doyle
Designer: Joanne Brown
Picture Manager: Cee Weston-Baker
Picture Researcher: Rachael Swann
DTP Manager: Nicky Studdart
DTP Coordinator: Sarah Pfitzner
DTP Operator: Primrose Burton
Senior Production Controller: Deborah Otter

Printed in Singapore

animal babies

in rain forests

My golden coat is covered in spots—it looks like I have flowers all over my back.

Who is my mommy?

My mommy is a jaguar, and I am her cub.

My mommy licks me with her bright pink tongue to keep me clean.

When there is danger, I stand up tall, beat my chest, and make a very loud noise.

Who is my mommy?

My mommy is a gorilla, and I am her infant.

We are such lazy apes that we like to sleep for most of the day.

My nose is a short trunk. I use it like a snorkel when I am in deep water.

Who is my mommy?

My mommy
is a tapir, and
I am her calf.

My baby fur is
stripy, but the
stripes will fade
as I grow older.

I like to **stare**, and the first things you will **see** are my **beady** eyes and their black **patches**.

Who is my mommy?

My mommy is a lemur, and I am her infant.

When we are out and about and my little legs get tired, my mom carries me on her back.

My **arms** are almost twice as long as my **legs**. They make it **easy** for me to **swing** through the trees.

Who is my mommy?

My mommy is an orangutan, and I am her infant.

When I am scared, I hold onto my mom so that I do not fall.

I have three sharp claws on my hands and feet. They help me hang upside down on branches.

Who is my mommy?

My mommy is a sloth, and I am her baby.

We are very slow and never hurry to go from here to there.

I have sticky pads under my feet. They help me sit on the branches of leafy trees.

Who is my mommy?

My mommy is a tarsier, and I am her infant.

We can turn our small heads almost all the way around, so I am never out of my mom's sight.

Additional Information

Although rain forests cover a very small area of the world—around seven percent—
an extraordinary variety of animals can be found there. They range from biting insects,
poisonous frogs, and snakes to butterflies as big as birds, exotic parrots, and large apes.
The animals in this book are found in various rain forests throughout the world—
jaguars, tapirs, and sloths are found in the large rain forests of Central and South America,
gorillas live in the African rain forest, lemurs can be found in northeast Madagascar,
orangutans in Southeast Asia, and tarsiers in the rain forests of Indonesia.

Acknowledgments

The publisher would like to thank the following for permission to reproduce their material.
Every care has been taken to trace copyright holders. However, if there have been
unintentional omissions or failure to trace copyright holders, we apologize and will,
if informed, endeavor to make corrections in any future edition.

Cover: Manoj Shah/Getty; Half title page: Masahiro Iijima/Ardea; Title page: Art Wolfe/Getty; Jaguar 1: Nick Gordon/Ardea;
Jaguar 2: Nick Gordon/Ardea; Gorilla 1: Art Wolfe Getty; Gorilla 2 Art Wolfe/Getty; Tapir 1: Tom Brakefield/Corbis;
Tapir 2: Slyvain Cordier/Ardea; Lemur 1: Adrian Warren/Ardea; Lemur 2: Adrian Warren/Ardea; Orangutan 1:
Manoj Shah/Getty; Orangutan 2: Slyvain Cordier/Ardea; Sloth 1: Jany Sauvanet/NHPA; Sloth 2: Kevin Schafer/Corbis;
Tarsier 1: Masahiro Iijima/Ardea; Tarsier 2: Patricia and Michael Fogden